Build, Grow, and Sell a

HIGH VALUE MANUFACTURING BUSINESS

Secrets to

Achieving Financial Independence by Building a Great Company

JEFF PALLISTER

Pallister Resource Management Ltd.
Est. 1973
Calgary, Alberta, Canada

Notice of Copyright

Copyright © 2021

Jeff Pallister

All rights reserved. No part of this publication may be reproduced, distributed or transmitted in any form or by any means, including photocopying, recording, or other electronic or mechanical methods, without the prior written permission of the publisher, except in the case of brief quotations embodied in critical reviews and certain other noncommercial uses permitted by copyright law. For permission requests, write to the publisher, addressed "Attention: Permissions Coordinator," at the address below.

Pallister Resource Management Ltd.
Box 19522 Cranston PO
Calgary, Alberta Canada T3M 0V4
https://www.highvaluemfg.com

Ordering Information:
Quantity sales. Special discounts are available on quantity purchases by corporations, associations, and others. For details, contact the "Special Sales Department" at the address above.

Printed in Canada
First Printing Edition, 2021
ISBN 9798709784413

Table of Contents

Introduction 1

1. Financial Independence 9

2. Optimal Timing 17

3. The Right Buyer 23

4. The Accelerated Growth Plan 31

5. Mobilize 39

6. The 10 Top Mistakes 49

7. Conclusion 55

Introduction

Achieve Financial Independence by Building a Great Company

You've invested considerable time, energy, and money into your business and made many sacrifices to achieve the success you have today. You deserve to get the best return on this investment you can: Financial Independence.

I wrote this book for business owners of manufacturing firms who want to build a great company that is more profitable, easier to run and is well-positioned to maximize the sales price when the owner decides to sell the business.

On its sale the owner achieves his or her end goal: financial independence.

But achieving financial independence can be difficult. There's many tough problems to resolve, major obstacles to overcome and a lot of work to do.

Cracking the Code

Early in my management consulting career, I started working with a rapidly growing company manufacturing factory-built buildings. The firm had a good product. Their market was expanding, and the owners were pursuing exciting growth opportunities. They called me in to help build their business to support its growth. They emphasized the stakes were high. The growth opportunities were real, but only if they could overcome their significant "growing pains".

Their growth consumed available cash putting enormous pressure on its limited resources. The firm lacked money, time, people and skills needed to support growth. This created a growing backlog of unresolved issues with customers, employees, and shareholders. Growth overwhelmed operations and they had problems with product quality and delivery.

Introduction

Everyone was frustrated. The company was in fire-fighting mode. There was a lot of drama and heroics. The company could not grow. It needed to overcome is various issues or lose out on its opportunities.

As I worked with the company, progress was slow at first. Getting commitment to building the business was difficult. I encountered significant resistance.

We had false starts and several employees didn't want to participate – they just wanted to get back to their "real work". Many people were impatient for results. There was a lot of pressure on staff to just work harder and faster. But that was counter-productive – it just made things worse.

During the day I'd work with staff on the tough issues. We'd try out different approaches to solving the problems. After work hours and on the weekends, I'd study how other companies resolved these types of issues and then apply these solutions to find out what worked and what didn't.

Working with management, we developed a growth plan and started mobilizing the organization to implement the plan. I put a special effort into finding how to make change happen with limited resources and in doing so, discovered the many assets hidden in the firm.

We set aside 3 hours every week with four different teams to work on the business. We ventured into the unknown and worked hard, even though we weren't certain whether we would be successful. We made some small changes.

One of the firm's hidden assets I found was in the brainpower of its people. Most people were hired for specific skills as operators or trades, but they had much more to offer. We tapped into their ideas about the work they and others did, what the problems were and how to fix the problems.

Every week we made progress on addressing the issues. This gave us a sense of momentum. Employees were engaged.

We made a breakthrough when a team identified over $40,000 of cost savings. When we presented the results, top management was skeptical. But we had hard evidence to back up our claims.

When management saw that the results were real, everything changed. They said, "give us more". We set up more teams tasked with building the business to support growth. Each team delivered on average over $50,000 worth of permanent changes to the business within a few months. In the next 18 months I worked with 16 more teams to resolve the company's most pressing issues.

Soon after I completed my assignment, another company acquired the manufacturing firm. The original owners received a premium price and had a successful exit.

Refine and Repeat the Success

Since this assignment, some 30 years ago, I've repeated this approach with several manufacturing firms. I've continued to develop, refine and implement a systematic approach to build and grow a high value manufacturing business.

With each company I worked with we first ensured they had a strong foundation in standardized work to achieve consistent results, increased efficiency and higher productivity.

We then created a "chain reaction" of events in each work area:

- make the work easier to do
- to make better quality products
- and get work done faster
- with less cost and risk
- which delights your customers who buy more product at a premium price,
- and your reputation attracts new customers.

This approach got great results: the business was easier to run, had higher margins and revenues grew.

Once the company gained consistency of operations and results and had established its own "chain reaction" of results, we expanded the scope of the improvement projects. We now sought out new opportunities: new products, new markets, new business models and new ways of working.

We continued to work with limited resources by finding and using hidden assets in the business, including the intellectual capital of employees, and other intangible assets. We worked with companies to strengthen the 18 key factors that generate improved performance and the value of a business. These are called "business drivers".

We've kept the business owners' end goal in mind: achieving financial independence. We do this by building and growing a great business that runs really well, is more profitable and that is positioned well to get them the maximum sale price when they choose to sell their company. When the owners sell their business, they unlock the full value and have financial independence.

In many ways, things haven't changed from my initial consulting assignment. The stakes remain high. Companies need to be more efficient and get consistent results, but they also have numerous growth opportunities that require different type of changes. With every industry now being disrupted every few years, few companies will thrive by only increasing the efficiency of their operations. They must seize new opportunities and make fundamental changes.

They still must resolve the twin issues of "growing pains" and limited resources. The breakthroughs come when the company finds its considerable **hidden assets** and uses these assets to building the company to support its growth and increase its value.

The High Value Manufacturing Business is a highly effective growth system you install in your business.

This system works so well because it creates more value for customers, more value from your operations and more value for shareholders. And it reduces the investments needed to grow your business by finding and using the considerable hidden assets in your business. It goes beyond quick fixes, simple cost-cutting and optimizing parts of the business.

In this book, I'm going to lay out a roadmap for you to increase the value of your firm to you as the owner. The result is that your company is more valuable to buyers and investors. You can then sell your firm at a higher amount than selling it "as-is". You can achieve this by accelerating the growth of your firm.

The bottom line: getting the full value for your business takes time and work but the rewards can far exceed the investment. The financial risk is reduced significantly when you fund your growth from hidden assets you already own but aren't using. It's like investing with "house money".

I wrote this book to give you an alternative to selling your business "as-is". Within a relatively short time, you can build your firm into an attractive acquisition that sells on your terms. You may not be selling your business in immediately, but you will be prepared to sell when you choose.

This book focuses on how you can achieve three key goals:

1. You sell your business at **your target price**, one that is significantly higher than its current, or "as-is" value.

2. You choose when to sell at **the optimal time** under any circumstance.

3. You sell your firm to **the right buyer**, the one who will make the company thrive and who shares your vision and values for the firm's future.

Introduction

This approach is not for every business owner, but is proven to work for:

- small manufacturing firms, having annual sales between $3 million and $25 million;
- entrepreneurial owners who are open to new ideas to grow their business and its value;
- owners who are impatient for results and can commit to take their company to its next level of performance.

I've discovered that there are really just three things you need to sell your business on your terms:

1. Focus on achieving a three key goals: your target value, the optimal timing, and the right buyer.
2. Have an Accelerated Growth Plan
3. Mobilize your organization to implement the Accelerated Growth Plan

That's it. You can sell your business on your terms. That's great news!

The High Value Manufacturing Business program works because it is focused on creating more value for your customers, more value from your operations, and by increasing shareholder value for owners. How does this work?

- When your business creates more value for your customers, revenues grow.
- When you create more value from your operations, your business is easier to run and you get higher margins.
- When you find hidden or underutilized assets and put them to work you minimize risks, have the resources to fund growth and you increase shareholder value.

As we go through this book, I'm going to show you an approach that takes your business to its next level of performance. It requires challenging conventional beliefs and replacing them with innovative thinking.

> *"The conventional view serves to protect us from the painful job of thinking." - John Kenneth Galbraith*

We've designed this program so that the Accelerated Growth Program:

- does not disrupt your business
- manages and limits risks
- gets rapid results, within 90 days
- is self-funding by making use of existing hidden assets
- has a minimum 5 times return on investment.

Let's get started.

Chapter 1
Financial Independence

The Three Things You Need

In the Introduction, I said there are just three things you need to do to sell your business on your terms:

1. Focus on achieving three key goals: your target value, the optimal timing, and finding the right buyer.
2. Have an Accelerated Growth Plan
3. Mobilize your organization to implement the Accelerated Growth Plan

Let's start with you're the first key goal: getting your Target Value and how you can get the best possible financial return on the investment you've made in your business.

Reaching your Target Value means you will be financially independent of your business, and free from the pressures of running a business. You can afford to enjoy life as you want, whether retirement, travel, a new venture, philanthropy, or other pursuits.

The Questions Needing Answers

You may ask many questions that leave you uncertain or even anxious about your future. You want to know:

- how much will I receive in net proceeds from the sale?
- will this be enough so I can be independent from the company? and
- what if the sale cannot support my financial goals?

The stakes are high. Many business owners have 80% or more of their net worth locked in their business. The sale must be successful. You need solid answers to these questions to reach your financial goals.

If the net proceeds are not high enough, or the sale is unsuccessful, you remain financially dependent on the business. It forces you to continue dealing with the pressures of running the business and you are not able to afford the lifestyle you expected.

You don't need to be uncertain about how to achieve your financial goals.

This chapter helps you gain greater clarity and certainty to achieve financial independence.

Challenge these Conventional Beliefs

Some business owners hold beliefs that prevent them from realizing the full value of their company. They believe that:

- their firm is worth more than it will realistically sell for
- they need to sell the business "as-is"
- they lack the resources needed to grow.

Merger and acquisition professionals report that business owners overestimating the value of their business is the number one reason for deals failing to close.

Most business owners do not plan and prepare their business for sale. They believe they have taken the firm as far as they can or are comfortable with. They want to sell their business as it is.

The third mistaken belief is that the business owner lacks the resources needed to grow their business and increase the value of the business before offering the company for sale.

Once you challenge these beliefs, you are free to increase the value of your company.

How to Achieve Your Target Value

Rather than accept the current value of your firm, let's focus on how to get your "Target Value". Target Value is the amount you are aiming to achieve.

The first decision to make is will you sell your business "as-is" or will you increase its value first?

CLOSE THE VALUE GAP

Let's first determine the "Value Gap". This is the difference between what your company's value is "as-is" if sold today, versus your target value.

When we conduct a "Discover" session with us, you see how an investor values your company and what areas of the business you need to improve its performance to reach your target value.

We use 18 business drivers to evaluate business performance. If you think of your business as an engine that generates results, your business engine has several gears that drive the business forward. We evaluate the performance of these gears or "business drivers".

ELIMINATE RED FLAGS

Some business drivers may have "Red Flags". These can cause a buyer to pass over your business immediately.

Suppose a company has ongoing litigation or has poor financial records. Both would create red flags and not only reduce the value of your firm, but it would scare away interested buyers. Any of the business drivers can have a status of red flag.

GROW YOUR BUSINESS

After red flags, we discover underperforming business drivers. When you strengthen these drivers, you grow your business and increase its value.

You may be reluctant to invest more time, energy, and money into your company. You've built the business to a certain level. Further growth requires more resources and added risk. Besides, new owners will have their own ideas and can risk their own money.

Let's challenge the assumption that growth adds too much investment and risk and keep in mind the large potential return on this investment.

INCREASE VALUE WITH HIDDEN ASSETS

Every company has many hidden assets and capabilities that are the key to increasing the value of our firm. These hidden assets also provide many of the resources needed to fund growth. You just need to know where to look for these hidden assets, increase their value and use the increased cash flow to build and grow your business.

One place to look for hidden assets is the cost of sales. Small manufacturers (having annual sales between $5 million and $25 million) have an average cost of sales of 69.4% of total revenue. The top tier firms have a cost of sales of 58.4%, a difference of 11%! Comparing net profit/loss figures reveal a 5.5% on average of manufacturers compared with 19.9% of top tier companies, a difference of 14.4%

Cost of sales is only one of many sources of hidden assets within your firm.

The differences between your firm and top tier firms can reveal a significant opportunity to increase the value of your firm.

It also gives you the opportunity to fund growth.

Accessing hidden assets provides the shortest path to getting a premium price for your business and realize your Target Value. We will provide more explanation of these hidden assets in Chapter 4–Accelerated Growth Plan.

An Example of Accelerating Growth

When I started working with a manufacturer of high-tech chemical sampling equipment and services, they had 32 highly qualified scientists, engineers, and technologists.

Their business was a "diamond in the rough". It had considerable expertise, delivered high value custom solutions, and its customers were happy. But it was difficult to scale the business. Like most companies, they hit a ceiling in their growth without having to make large investments and take on more risk.

They needed a fresh approach to develop more effective sales and operations. The company embarked on an intensive accelerated growth plan focused on a strengthening a few critical business drivers and mobilized the company to improve performance.

As the company made progress every quarter, revenues grew faster than expenses. The company reinvested profits in building the company. They used the increased cashflow to fund the company's growth.

In time, the company grew to 180 employees and gained 80% market share in its niche. It became an attractive investment target. The company was ready for investment, and a multinational firm acquired the company at a premium price.

The business owners had a successful business exit. I've worked with many other entrepreneurial manufacturing firms that have repeated this success using a proven model described later in this book.

Decide on Growth

Once you've determined not to sell your business "as-is" and want to sell it for a much larger target value, determine how to close the value gap between the two.

First determine the market value of your business "as-is". Next, determine the potential value of your firm by finding out the value of top tier companies in your industry.

At this stage you need a only a rapid assessment, conducted with minimal time and cost. Refer to "Next Steps" at the end of this book.

You can follow the rapid assessment with a Deep-Dive Analysis of your firm's 18 business drivers compared with top-tier firms. The Deep-Dive identifies your business strengths, weaknesses, and any "red flags".

Once you have a solid understanding of the business drivers, you can identify the top priority areas to improve with minimal risk and cost. You then add the target outcomes, activities, and resource requirements.

You now have a clear and direct path to achieving your financial goals, the first requirement of a successful business exit.

Action Plan

Take these actions to achieve your first key goal, Financial Independence:

1. Determine the actual value of your firm.
2. Determine the potential value of your firm.
3. Evaluate the performance of your firm's 18 business drivers.
4. Evaluate the changes needed to move your company towards its potential value.

5. Decide the target value of your company in one year.
6. Prepare a plan to close the gap between your firm "as-is" and your target value.

In the next chapter, we discuss the second key goal, finding the Optimal Timing.

Chapter Two
Optimal Timing

When do owners sell? I've heard several common answers from business owners, such as,

- "I'll sell when I'm ready,"
- "I'm going to sell when I reach age 65 (or other age)"
- "It's too early to tell, there's lots of time left,"
- "I'm going to keep on working until the company is worth more."

Even though many owners don't have a coherent exit plan, they do not want to leave it too late. Some say they will sell sooner than later for the right price. And others say they want more flexibility on timing.

The Problems with Vague Goals

Vague goals put the value of your company at risk under several scenarios:

- a highly motivated buyer is looking for a company in your industry, but there are too many other attractive choices
- unfortunate events occur - failing health, burnout, a recession, new competitors, products become obsolete, and so on
- your company is not growing - it is too early or too late in its growth cycle.

A Successful Exit Takes Time

Surveys conducted by the Exit Planning Institute found that 95% of business owners agreed with the statement, "Having a transition strategy is important for my future and the future of the business." Yet 61% of owners have given limited or no attention to their exit plans.

Other surveys found that many business owners realized after the sale that they should have increased the value of their business much earlier. Another study found that 75% of business owners profoundly regretted their decision to sell, mainly because of poor personal planning for their life after the sale.

It takes time to maximize the value of the business and become an attractive investment or acquisition.

If you wait until the last moment to sell your business, buyers may reject your business if it isn't ready for sale or isn't growing. You may regret leaving money on the table because you didn't leave enough time for growth.

In this chapter we provide an approach to optimizing the timing of the sale of your company. You don't have to settle for vague notions or goals.

Why not be ready to sell your business on your terms in one year, no matter when you intend to actually sell?

You will then be ready for the sale on your terms, regardless of circumstances - unfortunate events, encountering a rare golden opportunity from a motivated buyer, while positioning your company to sell when the market best meets your needs.

Beliefs Holding You Back

Three common beliefs concerning the timing of the sale prevent business owners from realizing the full value of their company:

1. "There's lots of time before the sale,"
2. "I'll prepare the company when it's time to sell,"
3. "In the meantime, it's business as usual–I don't have time to build the business."

I've been able to get better results by finding the optimal timing for the sale of a business. That way the owner is ready when opportunity knocks, is prepared for contingencies and can use the time now before the sale to grow their business.

Make the Most of a Golden Opportunity

Many of the most successful exits I've seen occurred because the business owners had prepared their business for sale and the right buyer arrived.

Motivated buyers can make generous acquisition offers in price and terms. You must be ready for these rare and unpredictable events. They may not come again. Even if you have no intention of selling today, you may receive a compelling offer tomorrow. Are you ready for a golden opportunity when it appears?

Be Ready for any Scenario

Any owner can encounter unfortunate events such as declining health, burnout, boredom, disruptive technologies, new competitors, market declines, pandemics and countless other issues that can force a sale.

The problem of ignoring these events is that when they occur, it may be too late to salvage the sale of the company on acceptable terms.

When you prepare your company for sale now, think of it as insurance and risk management. Be ready for these events and you and your firm can survive with a satisfactory exit under any circumstance or scenario.

Sell at the Right Stage of Growth

Investors look for companies at different stages of their growth. By finding the right type of investor, you can match your exit timing with the timing of their purchases.

Make Timing Flexible

I've replaced the conventional sales process and have much more flexibility. The usual sale scenario is the owner sells the business to a third party who helps with the transition for several months and moves on to other activities.

Instead, an owner can have a partial sale to "take some chips off the table." The owner continues to manage and control the business while managing the risks of owning a business.

Three Examples of Being Ready

My client was growing their business in prefabricated houses. An earthquake in Japan created an immediate and large demand for prefabricated houses. The client had a ready-made solution for a buyer. It was ready for sale. The deal closed quickly, and the owners made a successful exit.

Another client had built their business and captured a large market share in its niche in the oil and gas industry. Oil and gas prices jumped, and prices for companies rose as well. Buyers were bullish and sought acquisitions to grow their business. My client was well-positioned and made a successful exit. Their timing was excellent. They sold when the market was strong. Soon after the sale, the oil and gas market declined.

One company I worked with had developed proprietary electronic control products for industrial uses. Most buyers considered the firm too early for investment. It had annual sales of $2.5 million. Fortunately, the firm expected significant growth and prepared the company to scale up to meet demand.

A multinational company bought the firm. It had over 600 international sales offices and was able to increase sales of the acquired company by 10 times within two years through the buyer's international sales and distribution network.

Action Plan

Define the changes that you need to make if you had to sell your business one year from now.

In the next chapter, we look at the third key goal of selling a business on your terms: finding the right buyer.

Chapter Three
The Right Buyer

Some business owners are only interested in finding the buyer that offers the highest price. Owners who expand their criteria for finding their ideal buyer can get much better results.

Before putting your business up for sale, you can save time and energy by pre-qualifying buyers. Start off by screening out certain prospective buyers, ones that aren't able to close, don't have the right background, and who don't share your values.

Screen Out the Wrong Buyers

If you don't screen out prospective buyers, you may have an unpleasant experience as the buyer:

- gathers considerable confidential information on your firm
- wastes considerable time from management and staff
- disrupts operations
- takes too long in due diligence to make buying decisions.

I've used the following criteria to screen out the wrong buyers.

UNABLE TO CLOSE

If a buyer cannot close the right deal, they waste your valuable time and energy.

These buyers may lack access to adequate funding, review many deals, but close on very few. Some have very onerous terms and are only looking for bargain prices. Some even don't intend to close. Some are kicking tires, and some may be gathering competitive intelligence.

Avoid those potential buyers where you can't agree on the fundamental price and terms of the deal. Aside from price, ensure that you accept the financial structure, the source of funds, and the timeframe. You can establish this very early in the sales process, but you need to know your criteria.

WRONG BACKGROUND

Screen out buyers that don't have the right background. These prospective buyers lack focus on finding a specific type of business, don't have a defined price range, and don't have relevant business experience. This buyer will have difficulty adding value to your business.

THEY DON'T SHARE YOUR VALUES.

Screen out prospective buyers who don't share your vision and values. For example, you may want to ensure the continuity and growth of your business. You look for buyers that aim to keep your employees and not move the business.

Some may buy your business just to get your clients. They may not be interested in retaining staff or your facilities as they cut costs to gain short-term efficiencies and merge your business with another. Your legacy could be lost.

Ideal Buyer Criteria

Now you know what buyers you don't want; you can focus on the characteristics of an ideal buyer. You know that there needs to be the "right fit" between you and the buyer.

Early on, you can reach an initial agreement on approximate price and terms; you are confident in the buyer's ability to manage the business; and you both share common values and vision of the company after the sale.

In this chapter we identify the most important characteristics of an ideal buyer. In the last section, we provide some questions so you can apply these concepts to your business and develop the buyer profile.

THE RIGHT SKILLS AND BACKGROUND

The ideal buyer has a relevant background to your company. The buyer has worked with companies or owned business that resemble yours in the manufacturing industry with similar or larger size of revenues.

The right buyer's team has a strong background in manufacturing and operations and has hands-on management experience.

The ideal buyer has strong financial skills and a track record of acquisitions. The buyer can develop and negotiate the price and terms and can raise funds from investors and lenders.

The right buyer respects your time. The right buyer is efficient and effective and can close the right deal in a timely manner. The buyer has all the capabilities and resources needed to organize and close the deal. There are few hurdles to clear, and the buyer works quickly and simply while being rigorous.

The buyer knows what kind of deal they are looking for and communicates that early to you, the seller. The right buyer is innovative and flexible in terms. The right buyer works with you, not against you.

When you sell your company, you must be confident that competent and experienced leaders and managers will run the firm. They know how to transition from your company's current value to its desired value in the next 3 to 5 years.

These are diverse set of capacities skills rarely found in one individual. The buyer must be able to have or build a team with these skill sets.

A competent team is essential to ensuring a smooth transition and a successful business after the sale.

ABLE TO GROW THE BUSINESS

The ideal buyer is not only competent in managing your business with your help but should have a track record of growing revenues and cash flow. As the buyer evaluates your business, they develop a growth plan to grow the company and know how to mobilize the business to achieve the plan.

The key to having a deal that meets the needs of everyone is in creating a "bigger pie" for everyone. This is why an Accelerated Growth Strategy is important. I describe this strategy in the next chapter.

SHARES YOUR VISION AND VALUES

Many business owners are reluctant to sell their company to just any buyer. Owners have invested heavily into their businesses and want to see the business continue to operate, be well-managed and thrive.

A successful exit for the owner can include continued employment for staff, maintaining high quality standards, continuing to serve customers well, and continuing to give back to the community. These are all part of the business owner's legacy.

In most of the exits I've seen, the original owners made a successful exit and left their company stronger and in excellent hands. The company provided more opportunities for employees. The owners had made sure the buyer shared the owner's values.

The ideal buyer has the best interests of the company in mind. If business continuity, keeping employees, not moving the business are all important to you as an owner, make sure the buyer shares this vision of the firm.

Know the Buyer's Goals

Many buyers seek only the top tier companies, those in the top 25% of their industry as measured by growth, margins and cash flow. Other buyers look for "diamonds in the rough". These are good companies with solid growth prospects with management and investment.

Attract Strategic Buyers

Consider preparing your company for sale to a strategic buyer. A strategic buyer is a company in the same or similar line of business, such as a competitor or distributor. The reason the strategic buyer is interested in your company is that the purchase makes a significant difference to expanding their business. Your company is worth more than a part of their operations than it is as a stand-alone business.

For example, one company I worked with had $12 million in annual sales but was approached by a strategic buyer, was an international firm with annual sales of over $32 billion worldwide.

The small company's products and services added capabilities and customers to the multi-national firm. Within a few years the small firm had thousands of new customers. The buyer kept staff, made significant investments that grew the business and made the operations much stronger.

Motivated strategic buyers often pay a premium price for the right company.

An ideal buyer has the right background, ability to grow your business, and shared vision and values. You can use this checklist when selecting a broker or advisor.

By setting your criteria, you have immediately narrowed down the number of organizations you work with and know exactly who you are searching for.

Be proactive

Next, search for the right buyer, broker, M&A advisor or merchant banker. While some advisors cover many industries, look for specialists in the larger organizations, or work with small specialist firms.

I've found that the larger M&A firms focus on the sale of larger companies, those having annual sales greater than $30 million or even $50 million. Their advisory fees can be unaffordable for small companies intent on selling their business.

When you apply your criteria for the right advisor and buyer, you are focusing on fewer companies and individuals and can save an enormous amount of time. You will also get better and faster results by working with people who understand your industry and have the right background.

Evaluate the buyers

You interview candidates before hiring them. You qualify prospective suppliers. You also evaluate customers before doing business together. Take the same approach with a potential buyer of your firm.

By defining the ideal buyer, you can save yourself regrets of finding out later that the prospective buyer isn't a good fit and won't result in a successful deal.

Action Plan

1. Prepare a checklist of the most important characteristics of your ideal buyer, including:
    a. Background and experience,
    b. Track record in growing a manufacturing business,
    c. Values and vision for your company.

2. Start your search for potential buyers that meet your criteria, even if you are not planning to sell your firm immediately. It can take time to find and develop relationships with an idea buyer.

In the next chapter, let's review the most direct way to reach your Target Value using the Accelerated Growth Strategy.

Chapter 4
Accelerated Business Growth Plan

Sell Your Business "As-Is"?

Conventional Wisdom Makes Sense

Should you sell your business "as-is" or should you build up the value of the company before selling?

Selling your business "as-is" makes sense for many good reasons. You've taken the business as far as you feel comfortable. Building the company requires further investment, and there's no guarantee of a return. It increases your risks when you are trying to exit the business. It takes the least effort, time and risk. Besides, new owners will have their own ideas on the future direction of the company and can risk their own money.

Or Does It?

But it's not that simple. Before you make the decision to sell your company "as-is", answer these questions:

1. "how much money am I leaving on the table?"
2. "what needs to be done to reach my target value?"
3. "how much do I need to invest to reach the target value?" and
4. "what are the risks?"

Our approach is to capture a sizable portion of the full potential value of a business while minimizing the investment and risks.

The Accelerated Growth Plan

The key elements of the Accelerated Plan are:

1. Know Your Target Value
2. Define the Opportunities and Goals
3. Focus on Making the Right Changes
4. Run Self-Funded Projects
5. Manage the Risks
6. Increase the Multiple

Accelerated Growth provides a well-defined strategy and plan to achieve your Target Value while minimizing risks.

1. Know Your Target Value

Market, Target, and Potential Values

First, let's find out how much money you are leaving on the table. It is the difference between the "as-is" or current market value of your business and your target value. The market value is the amount a buyer will pay for your company "as-is".

Your target value is what you can reasonably expect to receive for your business after accelerated growth. Target value is more than market value, but less than its potential value.

The potential value is based on the performance and assets of top tier companies of similar size in your industry. Achieving top tier performance can require substantial investment and years of work. Our approach is to capture a large portion of the potential, but in a shorter time period and with less investment.

Discover Analysis

The Discover analysis is a primary tool to identify your firm's market value, its potential value, and the gap between the two. It also reveals the most important actions needed to close the gap. You then determine how much of that gap you want to close based on the size of the opportunity, the investment required, and risks involved.

You can easily find both these values with little time and effort using a simple "Discover" analysis. See "Next Steps" at the end of this book for more information.

2. Define the Opportunities and Goals

I've found that entrepreneurial manufacturing firms can set and achieve improvement targets amounting to:

- a 2-4% increase in annual revenues
- a 2-4% reduction in the cost structure, and
- a 1-3 point increase in the multiple.

When you combine these factors they compound the value of the company significantly.

These are "accelerated" targets above what the company has already set in its business plan. Many companies reaching these targets have doubled the value of their firm, and sometimes more, within one to two years.

3. Focus on Making the Right Changes

The "Discover" analysis identifies the most important business drivers that account for the gap between actual and potential business performance. The analysis allows you to estimate your target value at a high level. It also helps you identify "red flags" and "low hanging fruit". These are high priority business drivers that, when addressed, have high impacts relative to investments of time, energy, and money.

A more comprehensive guided and verified assessment, the "Deep-Dive", helps you understand and define the opportunities and targets more fully.

Independent value-added assessments that resemble due diligence but go beyond compliance and verification are also used to identify business improvements.

Accelerated Growth Workshops

I've found that one of the most productive ways to generate and evaluate specific improvements is through facilitated "Accelerated Growth Workshop".

One hidden and underutilized asset in most companies is the creative brainpower of its employees. During the Workshop, employees generate hundreds of improvement ideas and resources in less than a day. Once the ideas are generated, management evaluates the ideas and prioritize opportunities. The evaluation answers several questions:

- Which of these opportunities creates the greatest impact?
- How confident are we that this will achieve this impact?
- How easy is this opportunity to achieve?
- How much will it cost to make the needed changes?

Optimizing existing operations is simple common sense - it makes the most of what your company's assets.

Improvement Teams

One key to successful implementation of an Accelerated Growth Plan is to have the active participation of employees. Staff work within teams to uncover underutilized, untapped, and underperforming assets in the company. They are also responsible for implementing the changes needed to improve the performance of these assets.

4. Run Self-Funded Projects

Companies need resources including people, time, skills and money, to make the improvements leading to an increase in the value of their business.

Many of these changes can be self-funded. Fortunately, you can find these resources from operations. The key is to discover the hidden assets within your company.

We use the combination of tools - the Discover and Deep-Dive Analysis, Improvement Workshops and Improvement Teams to make the Accelerated Growth Program self-funding.

Several entrepreneurial manufacturing firms I've worked with have each generated several hundreds of thousands of dollars.

Individual Improvement Teams typically implement a minimum of between $50,000 - $100,000 in revenue improvements and cost savings. Teams accomplish results within three months. These are with small firms; larger firms generate even larger amounts.

Once management sees these results from the first teams, they typically add more teams to continue increasing revenues, reducing costs and improving margins.

I've worked with firms that have had 20 teams that generated between $1 million and $2 million in sustainable, permanent improvements, all within less than 2 years.

They reinvest increased cash flow to continued improvement.

Several teams can run concurrently. Once the team has completed their work, other teams to work on the next improvement priority.

5. Manage the Risks

An accelerated growth program involves risks that need managing.

The first major risk is selling the business "as is", the result of leaving money on the table.

When you decide instead to accelerate business growth, you need to manage other risks:

1. incurring costs that do not add value or a return
2. implementation risks of improvement projects not achieving results
3. solving the wrong problems
4. providing the wrong solutions

But before you proceed with these projects, prepare a Roadmap to define more precisely the work to be accomplished and address these risks.

The Roadmap Project

The Roadmap project specifically anticipates and minimizes the risks in growing a business. It addresses the following potential issues.

Costs. Changes can take longer and are more expensive than expected. Many companies don't know what changes they need to make, which changes make the biggest impact, and what the changes will cost.

Scope. The project Roadmap clearly defines the activities of the project and includes controls to keep the project on track.

Skills. The company may lack the skills to get the job done itself. It can bring in specialists. But even specialists may waste time and money and not achieve the desired results.

Implementation. One obstacle, for instance, is getting employee engagement and acceptance of changes. Even after changes have been identified, a company may struggle to keep the changes versus reverting to the old way of doing things. An improvement project can be risky. You do not get the results you wanted and end up with a poor or negative return on your investment. These risks can be managed and avoided.

6. Increase the Multiple

Buyers are particularly interested in the intangible assets of the companies they consider purchasing. Many of these intangibles are not identified on your financial statements as assets or earnings. But they have a large impact on the multiple on earnings assigned to the company and directly affects the price the buyer will pay.

A buyer wants to know the investments made in building and growing the existing business and what additional investments are needed to make the company perform as a top tier company.

This investment includes tangible assets such as equipment, and inventory and intangibles such as the business infrastructure, which includes assets found within the company's knowledge, people, customers and management system.

Companies caught up in the "whirlwind" of the daily operations may not be investing much back into their company. I've heard managers say they don't have the time, energy, money or skills needed to build the business any further than absolutely necessary. A buyer could see this business as a depreciating asset that may require significant investments to be competitive.

Investments into the business impact the company's earnings, which directly affect the value of the company. The intangible assets are significant and can account for 50% or more of a company's value.

Tap into hidden assets.

Manufacturing companies can optimize their operations with significant results. The average manufacturing firm cost of sales is 11% higher than those firms in the top quartile. The initial aim could be to capture only one quarter of that difference within one or two years. And that is only one area of the business that can be optimized. We look at all 18 business drivers to find improvements.

The aim is to improve sales and operations by making improvements that make work easier, produces better products, gets work done faster and at lower cost. This translates into increased customer satisfaction, retention, and higher margins. The result is a growth of the business and its value.

Action Plan

Prepare Your Accelerated Growth Plan, including these sections:

1. Target Value
2. Opportunities and Goals
3. The Workplan
4. Self-Financing Plan
5. Risk Management
6. Increase the Multiple

Chapter 5

Mobilize

Overcoming the Obstacles

Owners encounter several issues to growing their business: it takes too much time, it's too disruptive, it's too expensive, and too risky.

Too busy. The day-to-day demands from customers and employees leave little time and energy left to conduct new improvement initiatives.

Too disruptive. Changes can disrupt operations and can create more problems than they solve.

Too expensive. Bringing in people from the outside for advice can mean large costs. There are expenses for employees in training and lost productive time. These costs don't always make sense, especially if they don't produce lasting results.

Too risky. Even with a good plan, there's no guarantee of getting desired results, putting the investment of time, energy and money at risk.

Adapt and Change

Despite these issues, an owner may not want to sell the business "as-is". These issues can be addressed and minimized. The investment can be worthwhile if they produce a high return. The return we are aiming for is profitable business growth that increases the value of the business. This allows you to receive your Target Price.

While owners and management remember past disappointments in growing their business, they also have conducted successful projects. Perhaps it was developing an improved product, entering a new market, winning a new account, or installing new information technologies. Companies do not stand still. They adapt and make changes to survive and thrive.

Once a company has developed its growth plan, the big challenge is implementing the plan successfully. In my experience, companies find implementation is much more difficult than planning. Even if with a great plan, initiatives fail to achieve their results because of implementation issues.

Before getting underway, be prepared to address three major causes of unsuccessful improvement initiatives.

- The demands of day-to-day activities
- Lack of buy-in and support by employees
- No method to follow

Daily-to-Day Demands

The day-to-day demands on a company can easily crowd out time and energy. The story about "sharpening the saw" comes to mind. A woodcutter was struggling to saw down trees. Despite working hard for several hours, he was not making progress and was getting exhausted. A young man said, "if you sharpen your saw, you could cut the trees much faster. The woodcutter explained, "I don't have time to sharpen the saw. Don't you see I'm too busy?"

While there never seems to be a good time to improve a business. Owners often encounter resistance to change. I've heard managers and employees say they want to minimize the time spent on improving the business, so they can get back to their "real work". But improvement work makes the "real work" easier, gets better results, and takes less time.

It requires a commitment to set aside the resources–especially people and time - to invest in the company to sharpen the saw.

Lack of Buy-in

It's natural for people to feel comfortable following regular work routines, and they may resist changes as being too disruptive.

When companies rely too much on managers and outside experts in solving problems, they risk project failure. Sometimes only a few people determine what the business problems are, their causes, and the solutions. Then the experts don't involve people actually doing the work.

Management then imposes the new way of doing things But the people actually doing the work may not know the reason for the changes and may disagree with the solutions.

The result is that the people doing the work don't take responsibility for the results, and the changes don't last.

Employee participation is essential for getting the best results and to ensure staff support and buy-in. I've found that some of the best experts to improve the business are the people doing the work. Employee participation is also key to building a company that can run without the owners, a key factor in selling a business.

Uncertain results

Another cause of project failure is the lack of a systematic method for making changes. Not using a proven method has serious consequences:

- results are unpredictable
- some areas of the business are improved but create problems in other areas of the business
- employees and managers are frustrated when they don't know what to do or how to do it and don't have support in implementation.

These issues lead to negative attitudes and resistance to change.

The Goal is Predictable Growth

Increasing a company's value is achieved by a having predictable growth in revenues, cash flow and equity value. I've found that the best approach is to:

- set the right target value
- focus on making the right changes
- make use of readily available resources
- minimize the risks.

The result is a high return on investment, the increased value of your business. A substantial amount of the investment can be self-funded and is accomplished while minimizing risks. I've found that some of the biggest wins come from increasing the value of hidden, intangible assets. Intangible assets need to be transferable during the sale of the business.

Intangible assets

Your company's most valuable assets may not appear your financial statements. The balance sheet lists physical assets such as land, buildings, equipment, inventory, cash and accounts receivables. But every company has other valuable intangible assets found in the company's knowledge, people, customers and management system.

In the past, the physical assets created wealth. But increasingly, intangible assets are becoming equally or even more important than physical assets of a company.

KNOWLEDGE

Knowledge assets and intellectual capital are among the most important intangible assets. These assets are the talents, skills and know-how of a company's people and in its processes, methods, and formulas used to produce its products and services. Buyers will often pay a premium for proprietary products, patents, trademarks, or copyrights. Knowledge assets need to be transferable during a sale. The knowledge of owners needs to be captured and transferred into the organization. Otherwise, the company will not be able to run effectively for the new owners.

One of the most under-utilized and hidden assets within a company is its intellectual capital found in the brainpower of its employees. Our approach relies on this resource to find the opportunities in the company through Accelerated Growth Workshops.

PEOPLE

Developing a firm's people is one of the greatest opportunities to grow a business and its value. Buyers evaluate a company on the tenure, experience, and credentials of its people. They look for a strong and vibrant culture and people who accept new challenges.

Yet, according to a recent survey, the most important current issue facing privately held businesses is labor availability.

CUSTOMERS

Buyers are keenly interested in the strength of a company's customer base intangible assets, such as agreements, relationships, goodwill, and loyalty. The relationships will need to be transferable from one owner to another.

Buyers also evaluate the diversity of a company's customer base. Too much concentration on a few customers is a risk to a buyer, even though long-term agreements may be in place. A buyer will pay a premium to access a solid, loyal and customer base. A successful transition requires that business owners can transfer customer intangibles, such as established relationships, to the new owners.

MANAGEMENT SYSTEM

A company's management system is the business infrastructure supporting operations. It has been described as "how we do the work". This includes its policies, processes, procedures, resources, technology, and facilities to achieve its objectives.

Buyers evaluate a company's management system by its maturity and transferability to new owners. Less mature systems have inconsistent, uncoordinated processes. As the systems mature, processes become more controlled, coordinated, streamlined and transparent. Systematized processes reduce waste and improve quality. This improves customer satisfaction and retention. All have positive impacts on growth in revenues, cash flow and value.

A more mature management system makes a company easier to run, easier to grow, and more transferable to a new owner. The company can run effectively and efficiently without the owners.

Future Value

A common warning phrase for stock market investors is "past performance is no guarantee of future results". This warning applies to private companies for sale.

A growth formula that has worked in the past may not work in the future. Markets are disrupted with greater frequency from technology, globalization, competition, and regulations, buyers will value your company on how well it is positioned to survive and thrive into the future.

Adapt or Perish

Every thriving company can adapt to changing conditions and renew itself. The most successful strategies rely on tapping into a company's hidden assets. These are assets the company has already or can easily access buy are undervalued, unrecognized or undervalued.

One of these hidden assets is your company's capabilities, where the company invests in a few core capabilities that focus on capabilities that are at the center of competitive success. Companies have found renewal through improving its cost position, quality, and improving speed.

As an example, a manufacturer of doors and windows determined that its customers would shop for products and decide on how fast a supplier would have the products built and delivered. The company's average turnaround time was 45 days. Management focused on building the company's capabilities to reduce turnaround to 11 days, established itself as an industry leader, and gained market share.

Repeatable

You can join the top tier companies in your industry by accessing intangible assets, building future value, and then developing a repeatable business model. Your firm's competitive strengths, when combined, can be its most valuable assets.

I've found small manufacturing companies achieve significant growth by optimizing operations. They create a chain reaction of events:

- make work easier to perform
- this creates more consistent results and
- reduces defects and waste
- the result is faster results, improved quality, lower costs
- which results in increased customer satisfaction and retention

Combining this sequence of strengths creates more predictable revenue growth, margins, and cash flow.

Predictable growth

Valuing a manufacturing firm is heavily weighted to past performance, and future projections are often not used or are discounted.

Buyers are investors in the future and are keenly interested in a company's future prospects. The better the outlook, the higher the multiple and value of your company.

You can increase the multiple with a combination of accessing intangible assets, building the future value of the firm, and having a repeatable business model focused on key competitive strengths.

When you combine these drivers, you are reducing the risk of the investment by creating more predictable results in growing revenue, cash flow, and equity value.

Recap: The Steps to Reaching Target Value

In working with many manufacturing firms, I've found that the major steps to reaching the owner's target follow a well-defined sequence. The two major steps are to create the Accelerated Growth Plan and then Mobilize the organization to implement the Plan.

To recap, the steps leading to the Accelerated Growth Plan are to:

- identify the value gap
- generate ideas to close the gap
- evaluate the ideas to identify the priority opportunities for improvement
- identify the resources required
- organize these into well-defined improvement projects
- prepare, communicate, and commit to a plan for accelerated growth

This provides you a clear understanding and plan of what needs to be done to close the value gap and increase the value of your business.

The biggest challenge

Once you have a plan to grow your company, your biggest challenge is to have your people implement the strategy.

This requires leadership in setting and communicating a clear vision of the changes and then making commitments to ensure its success.

The improvements will require allocation of resources to make the changes.

People need to set aside time to do the work. I've found ways to free up time that minimize time and costs and that do not disrupt operations. Be clear that the improvement work is just as important as their "real job", especially as people may say "we don't have time for this."

To ensure success, you want to follow a proven method to Mobilize to get the results you want and not leave people floundering because of lack of structure and organization.

A Proven Method

We've used and refined the following 7 step method since 1990 to get consistent and predictable results.

1. Initial Assessment
2. Comprehensive Assessment
3. Business Growth Strategy
4. Mobilization Plan
5. Mobilization
6. Monitor and Measure Results

7. Course Correction and Rollout to Other Areas

Repeat this cycle for continual improvement and achieving a "flywheel" growth cycle.

Mobilize

Given the right leadership and having people follow a proven method, you are now mobilizing your organization to strengthen the key business drivers that generate your company's competitive advantage and performance results.

The result of a well-run and high performing company is a higher multiple and value of your company.

Action Plan

Get started with the first 3 steps of the 7 Step Growth Method.

1. **Initial Assessment.** Conduct an initial assessment of your firm's strengths and weaknesses. The assessment allows a detailed discussion of the top three bottlenecks to growth and operational efficiency. It identifies the impact of these bottlenecks on the equity value for your business.

2. **Comprehensive Assessment.** Conduct a more comprehensive company analysis with key senior staff. For a detailed analysis of operations, think of this as a health scan of your entire business. This analysis will develop the understanding need to create your Growth Strategy.

3. **Growth Strategy.** Deliver the Strategy, with prioritize recommendations to strengthen your growth and equity value.

In the next chapter, we present the Top 10 Mistakes to avoid.

Chapter 6
The 10 Top Mistakes

1. NOT UNDERSTANDING WHAT THE BUYER VALUES

Some sellers present their company through their view of their company, not what the buyer is looking for. Buyers look for consistent and predictable earnings, both in the past and the company's potential to deliver future earnings. The buyer is looking at the intangible assets of the company and its value drivers–the functions of the business that generate these earnings. The buyer looks for opportunities for scalable growth and asks, "how can this business increase revenues, while controlling costs?" The buyer also asks, "how can I increase the multiple of this business" and "how can I make this company easier to run?"

The buyer will also look for a strong and cohesive management team. The company needs to have a growth strategy and the leadership and management to mobilize the organization to its next level.

Past performance of the company does not mean the company has a bright future. The firm needs to seize opportunities as markets and technologies change. An attractive acquisition finds new opportunities, has innovative products, works on process innovation, transfers in technology, and uses automation and current information technologies.

2. EXPECTING QUICK RESULTS

Many owners underestimate the time, and effort required to sell their business.

The company needs to document its track record of financial and operational results for at least the past 3 years. It may take a company many years to grow the company to achieve the valuation desired by the owner.

Once the business is investor-ready, the owner or broker needs to find and qualify suitable buyers, conduct negotiations with several buyers, and then complete the agreements. Unless there is an all-cash deal, the buyer will be an investor in the company until they pay the vendor note, up to 3 to 5 years after the purchase.

3. FAILING TO PLAN

Many sellers lack an exit plan that looks at all aspects of the owner's transition–personal, business, financial, legal objectives and how to achieve these objectives. The owner needs to prepare for contingencies. This exit planning work may involve working with several professional advisors– lawyers, accountants, tax experts, management consultants, human resource consultants, and wealth management planners. The stakes are high, and planning pays off. For example, tax planning can result in considerably less tax on the sale proceeds.

If an owner puts a business on the market before it is ready, it will lose opportunities with potential buyers.

The buyer is interested in potential future earnings that have a basis in a growth plan. This is one way of increasing the value of the business significantly. The plan identifies the opportunities, the management team, and organization that will deliver on the opportunities. It will also show how the company will build the infrastructure to scale the business, whether that is new products, new markets, staffing, procedures, equipment, and the resources needed to finance the growth.

4. LACKING FLEXIBILITY

When a seller sets an asking price, the buyer expects to understand the basis for the price. Ideally, the seller or broker has conducted a valuation of the business and shares the rationale with the seller. The buyer may value the company on other measures.

They may structure a deal in several ways and can offer great flexibility in meeting the needs of both buyer and seller. Payment may comprise a portion of cash on closing plus cash within the first year, a vendor note and an earn-out.

Owners may want to sell part of their company now to reduce risk to their net worth, but continue to be active in the business to take part in taking the company to the next level.

5. LACK OF MANAGEMENT SUCCESSION

One concern of a buyer is that the acquired company will lose momentum once the current owners leave. The transition could cause customers or employees to leave and the company going into decline. The business will need to run without the owners, and the new owners will need time to understand the business. The business may also lack capable management able to grow the company. New owners will have to recruit the right talent to build a cadre of people to implement the new owner's Growth Strategy.

6. POOR QUALITY OF INFORMATION

Buyers need to have accurate, up-to-date information on the business. This includes having current monthly financial statements prepared by a qualified accountant. It includes the financial, legal, and corporate information. Buyers expect this information to be readily available and it isn't, they may decline to pursue the acquisition of the firm.

7. LAST-MINUTE PREPARATIONS

When sellers prepare their business for sale, the financial statements can show a surge in sales and a spike in earnings in the last year. It appears there were a flurry of activities occurring that could be only short-term gains. But are they a reliable indicator of future performance? The results may not be sustainable, and the company may have exceeded its capacity through too many initiatives to prepare for the sale transaction.

8. WEAK SALES AND MARKETING

Some companies have established relationships with only a few key customers. This customer concentration may show that the company has weak marketing and sales and is at risk by relying on too few customers. A valuable company is constantly acquiring new customers and markets and diversifies its customer base.

9. WEAK MANAGEMENT SYSTEM

A company with a weak management system is difficult to evaluate during due diligence. A management system is a set of policies, processes and procedures used by a company to ensure that it fulfills the tasks required to achieve its objectives. Elements are wide ranging and include leadership, quality, health and safety, product standards, documentation, management of change, risk management. Companies with established management systems have internal audits that provide the buyer with information necessary for due diligence. Strong and mature management systems increase the value of intangible assets and directly affect the multiple paid for a company.

10. GETTING OVERWHELMED

Running a business is demanding. Add in the work needed to exit your business, and it is easy to become overwhelmed. The key is to have a well-defined strategy, a plan, and the ability to mobilize your organization to implement the plan. It also requires having a team of experienced advisors and work with the right buyers to transition successfully.

In the final chapter, we provide a brief recap of the Accelerated Growth Strategy, and the Next Steps you can take.

Chapter 7
Conclusion

In this book, we've presented an alternative approach to selling your business. By taking this approach you can make rapid progress on your major goals: financial independence, optimal timing, and selling to the right buyer.

The following table compares conventional strategy versus an Accelerated Growth Strategy.

Goal	Business Sale Strategy	
	Conventional	Accelerated Growth
Financial Value	Sell the business "as-is"	Sell for your Target Price
Timing	Focus on the transaction	Build the business at least 1 year before the sale
Timing	Vague or fixed date for transition	Optimal Timing – be ready to sell any time you choose and be ready for the right opportunity
Buyer	Best offer	Right Buyer - who has the relevant background and who shares your vision and values

Consider the sizable investment you've already made in your business when selling your business. Both the stakes and potential rewards are high.

The Accelerated Growth program can achieve a significantly higher return on your investment than conventional approaches. It works because it focuses on reaching three key goals: your target value, optimal timing, and finding the right buyer. And then it provides a plan and a method for accomplishing these goals.

CHAPTER 7. CONCLUSION

Next Steps

I hope this book has sparked some new thinking and insights for you. Whenever you're ready, here are two ways we can help:

1. Subscribe to **The Successful Manufacturing Business** podcast. https://highvaluemfg.com/podcast

2. Work with my firm to accelerate the growth of your business and increase its value. To find out if we are a fit, email me at jeff.pallister@highvaluemfg.com and put "work with me" in the subject line.

About the Author

Jeff Pallister is a management consultant, investor, and business owner. He is founder of the **High Value Manufacturing Business** Program, a highly effective system for companies to accelerate growth in revenues, cash flow and shareholder equity. He is the author of *Chain Reaction, The Executive's Action Plan for Turning Creativity and Teamwork into Sustainable Profits.*

For more information about the High Value Manufacturing Program: https://highvaluemfg.com

www.ingramcontent.com/pod-product-compliance
Lightning Source LLC
Chambersburg PA
CBHW030506220526
45464CB00006B/2683